16

Ple
Yo
or

CUSTO

History and activities of
Ancient Egypt

Alexandra Fix

www.heinemann.co.uk/library
Visit our website to find out more information about Heinemann Library books.

To order:
☎ Phone 44 (0) 1865 888066
    Send a fax to 44 (0) 1865 314091
📄 Visit the Heinemann Bookshop at www.heinemann.co.uk/library to browse our
 catalogue and order online.

First published in Great Britain by Heinemann Library, Halley Court, Jordan Hill, Oxford OX2 8EJ, part of Harcourt Education. Heinemann is a registered trademark of Harcourt Education Ltd.

Editorial: Audrey Stokes
Design: Kimberly R. Miracle in collaboration with Cavedweller Studio
Picture research: Mica Brancic
Production: Camilla Crask

Origination: Chroma Graphics
Printed and bound in China by WKT Company Limited

10-digit ISBN 0431080844
13-digit ISBN 9780431080840
11 10 09 08 07
10 9 8 7 6 5 4 3 2 1

British Library Cataloguing in Publication Data
Fix, Alexandra, 1950-
Ancient Egypt. – (Hands on ancient history)
1. Egypt – Civilization – To 332 B.C. – Juvenile literature
2. Egypt – History – To 332 B.C. – Juvenile literature
I. Title
932
A full catalogue record for this book is available from the British Library.

Acknowledgements
The author and publishers are grateful to the following for permission to reproduce photographs: Ancient Art and Architecture Collection, p. **12** (R. Sheridan); Bridgeman Art Library, pp. **18** (Egyptian National Museum, Cairo, Egypt, Giraudon), **22** (Louvre, Paris, France); Corbis, pp. **4** (Roger Wood), **7** (Archivo Iconografico, S.A.), **9** (North Carolina Museum of Art), **10** (Burstein Collection), **11** (Bettmann), **8**, **13** (Sandro Vannini), **14**, **26** (Gianni Dagli Orti), **15** (Werner Forman), **16** (Archivo Iconografico, S.A); Harcourt, pp. **17** (David Rigg), **21** (David Rigg), **25** (David Rigg), **29** (David Rigg).

Cover photographs of a painting of an Egyptian king and queen (foreground) reproduced with permission of Alamy Images/Worldwide Picture Library and the Sphinx (background) reproduced with permission of Getty Images/Photodisc.

The publishers would like to thank Emily Teeter, Eric Utech and Kathy Peltan for their assistance in the preparation of this book.

Every effort has been made to contact copyright holders of any material reproduced in this book. Any omissions will be rectified in subsequent printings if notice is given to the publishers.

Contents

Some words are shown in bold, **like this.** You can find out what they mean by looking in the glossary.

The River Nile flows through Egypt. More than 7,000 years ago people farmed along its banks. They built homes on higher ground near by. There were settlements in the north, called Lower Egypt, and in the south, called Upper Egypt. These regions were united around 3000 BCE. Their first **pharaoh** was King Menes, also known as King Narmer. Egyptian life centred around this **fertile** Nile valley. But the valley made up only ten per cent of the country. A hot, dry desert covered the rest of the land.

The Nile valley was called the "Black Land" because of its dark soil. The desert was called the "Red Land" because of the sun's reflection on the hot sands.

Timeline

Egyptians use hieroglyphs **3000 BCE**		Assyrians control Egypt **671 BCE**

| People settle near the Nile **5500 BCE** | Egypt unites and first pharaoh rules **3000 BCE** | First pyramid is built **2700 BCE** | Persians rule Egypt **525 BCE** |

Flooding and farming

Every year in July, the River Nile overflowed its banks. The waters flooded the surrounding land for four months. By November, flooding stopped and the ground began to dry out. The waters left behind sticky, black mud that was good for growing crops. Next came the planting season. Farmers used oxen to plough the fields. They scattered seeds by hand while the ground was still wet. In May the crops were gathered and stored. By July flooding began again. It was important that the river flooded each year. Without the rich soil left behind, crops would not grow well. The people might starve.

Greeks conquer Egypt
332 BCE

Romans conquer
Egypt **30 BCE**

Cleopatra VII is the last Egyptian queen
51 BCE

About dates

The phrases BC and BCE show that something happened before Jesus was born. The phrases CE and AD show that something happened after Jesus was born. On this timeline you can see that Rome conquered Egypt 30 years before Jesus was born. With modern dates we do not usually use CE or AD. Everyone assumes we are talking about today.

The gifts of the Nile

The Nile is the longest river in the world. It is about 6,671 kilometres (4,145 miles) long. Its main source is Lake Victoria in modern-day Uganda. The Nile flows north through Egypt and empties into the Mediterranean Sea.

Upper Egypt developed to the south, or upstream. Lower Egypt was settled in the north, where the river empties into the Mediterranean Sea.

The ancient Egyptians lived and worked along the banks of the river. They also lived along streams that branched out from the Nile. The river gave them water for drinking, bathing, and watering crops. The river kept the soil **fertile**. Crops grew well. There were fish, birds, and other animals nearby for food.

The river also helped in other ways. River mud could be formed into bricks to build homes. A plant, called flax, grew along the Nile. Flax could be woven into cloth. The river was also a source of **papyrus**. Papyrus was a type of river reed. It could be made into paper, rope, cloth, sandals, baskets, mats, boats, and rafts. The Nile provided all that was needed. Egypt became a strong, independent nation.

Egyptian rulers

Powerful kings, called **pharaohs**, governed Egypt. People believed that the pharaohs were like gods. Most pharaohs were men, but not all. Queen Hatshepsut ruled for 21 years. She dressed like male pharaohs. Tutankhamun became king at the age of nine. He died when he was only eighteen.

Until 1000 BCE, rule by pharaohs was strong. After that, Egyptians were controlled by the Assyrians and Persians. Later, Alexander the Great conquered Egypt for Greece. After Alexander's death, one of his generals became king. Cleopatra VII was a **descendant** of that general. She became the last queen of Egypt. Egypt was defeated by the Romans in 30 BCE. It became part of the Roman Empire.

This gold funeral mask was found in the tomb of Tutankhamun in 1922. Historians believe that this is what the boy-king looked like.

7

Egyptian writing

Egyptians were some of the first people to have a written language. They used a type of writing called hieroglyphics. Symbols and pictures stood for objects and sounds. Later, the symbols became simpler. They looked more like cursive writing. These later styles were called hieratic and demotic.

Sometimes hieroglyphs were carved into the walls of tombs and temples. Sometimes they were written on **papyrus** with a brush and ink. Papyrus pages could be pasted together to form a scroll. Egyptians wrote down records of important events. They also recorded everyday life. Because the people wrote so much down, we know many details of Egyptian life.

The Rosetta Stone was discovered In 1799. This stone had the same story written in three languages. It was written in hieroglyphs, demotic, and Greek. The Greek words helped scholars to translate the Egyptian words. The Rosetta Stone helped scholars understand the meaning of the hieroglyphs.

 The Step Pyramid at Saqqara was designed by Imhotep, the first architect whose name was ever recorded.

Pyramid tombs

The Egyptians built tombs and monuments of stone. These buildings honoured the **pharaohs**. The Step Pyramid at Saqqara was one of the earliest stone buildings ever made. Egyptian workers built it without using cranes, pulleys, or wheels!

Growing and gathering

There was not much rain, so Egyptians had to **irrigate** their crops. They dug **canals** to bring water closer to the fields. They also invented a machine called the *shaduf*. A bucket was put into the water. A lever with a weight on the end lifted the full bucket to water the fields. Irrigation is still important in Egypt today.

The Egyptians knew many things about growing and gathering plants. They also kept bees and collected honey. Honey was used for food and medicine.

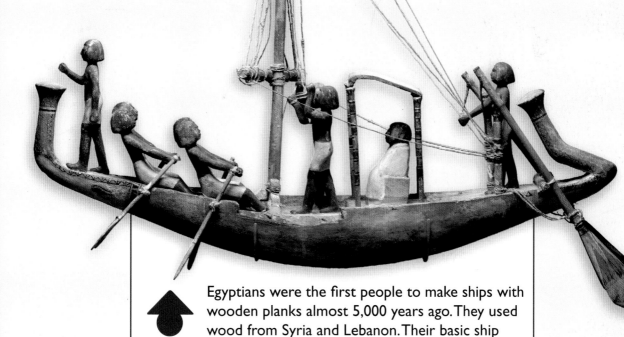

Egyptians were the first people to make ships with wooden planks almost 5,000 years ago. They used wood from Syria and Lebanon. Their basic ship design is still used today around the world.

Chapter 2: Egyptian families and communities

Family life was important to ancient Egyptians. Young girls helped their mothers in the home. Boys learned to work with their fathers. Girls and boys married in their teens. Families were big, and some had 15 children. Most Egyptians died by their mid-30s.

Husbands and wives were equal, but they had different roles in the family. Women cooked and cleaned. They cared for the family and made clothing. They also made things to trade. Women could have jobs outside the home. They could be weavers, servants, bakers, musicians, and dancers. They could also own and sell property.

In ancient Egypt, parents, children, grandparents, and other relatives often lived together in the same home.

There were more than 2,000 gods and goddesses in ancient Egypt. Each one was in charge of a different part of life or death. Ancient Egyptians worshipped in private and in public. Prayers and sacrifices were offered to the gods.

More than 50 pyramid tombs were built in ancient Egypt.

Duty work

When a pharaoh began a building project, thousands of workers were needed. Peasants had to work a certain number of hours each year for the pharaoh. This was called duty work. Most duty work was done during flood season. Farmers could not work in the fields when they were flooded.

Social classes

A man's work decided his place in society. That did not usually change. Sons were expected to do the same work as their fathers. Education and military service were the only ways to move up. Most Egyptians were **peasants**. They worked as farmers, fishermen, and servants. Skilled craftspersons, soldiers, and merchants had more status. Scribes, priests, doctors, and engineers were very important people. The **pharaoh** was considered the most important. Slaves had the lowest social status.

Egyptian food, clothing, and shelter

Bread was the most basic part of an Egyptian meal. It was made from a type of wheat and barley. A drink was made from fermented barley. A typical meal might be bread, an onion or other vegetable or fruit, and a barley drink. Meat was not eaten often. But when it was, it was usually fish, duck, or wild bird.

Peasants wore linen cloths tied around the waist and simple shirts. The upper class wore white linen robes. Sandals were made of **papyrus**. Men and women had different hairstyles. For special occasions, they wore wigs made of human hair. Children wore a sidelock. Both men and women wore bracelets, necklaces, and beaded collars. They also used an eye make-up, called kohl, around their eyes.

This clay model of a family's home is called a soul house. It would have been put in a person's tomb.

We have learned many things about the life and customs of the ancient Egyptians from scenes like this, painted on the inside walls of pyramids and tombs.

Ordinary Egyptian homes were made of mud brick. They were small and simple. There was an entryway, living room, sleeping room, and storage space. Most were only one storey high. Meals were cooked in an outdoor courtyard or on the roof. There were low tables and woven mats for seats. Beds were often simple mats.

Getting around in Egypt

Egyptians walked almost everywhere. They used rafts or boats on the river for longer distances. There were no other vehicles ordinarily used. There was a carrying-chair used for officials and the queen or the **pharaoh**. Chariots were used only for military or hunting expeditions.

Chapter 3: Egyptian fun

Boys and girls of ancient Egypt enjoyed running, jumping, and playing ball games. Children played leapfrog, tug of war, and hopscotch. Boys played with marbles and wooden spinning tops. Girls loved dolls and dressed them in simple doll's clothes. Board games, especially snake and senet, were popular among children and adults.

Egyptians swam in the Nile. They hunted wild animals and birds for sport. Another popular sport was wrestling.

The serpent game was played on this spiral circuit with marbles and pieces in the form of lions.

Entertainment

Many Egyptians enjoyed music and dance. Most entertainers were women. Favourite instruments were pipes, flutes, harps, tambourines, drums, and cymbals. Men and women did not usually dance together. Egyptians also liked to tell stories about their history and gods.

Wealthy Egyptians often enjoyed fancy parties with lots of things to eat and drink. Men and women wore their finest clothes to these parties.

This female lute player might be entertaining at a banquet or public festival.

More than a pet

The Egyptian Mau cat was tamed from an African wild cat. Modern housecats are **descendants** of the cats of ancient Egypt. Cats were kept as pets, but they also had important jobs. They killed poisonous snakes from the river. They kept rats and mice away from stored grain. Egyptians loved cats so much that they created and honoured a cat goddess. She was named Bastet.

By doing the hands-on activities and crafts in this chapter, you will get a feel for what life was like for people who lived and worked in ancient Egypt.

Recipe: Tiger nut sweets

Tiger nut sweets were a popular dessert served at a feast or celebration. This is one of the oldest recorded recipes. The original recipe was actually found written on a broken piece of Egyptian pottery, called *ostraca*. **Papyrus** was expensive, but *ostraca* was like scrap paper.

Ingredients

- 12 dried dates, pits removed
- 65 g walnut pieces
- 125 ml honey
- ½ tsp cinnamon
- 400 g ground almonds

(Make sure no-one eating these sweets has a nut allergy).

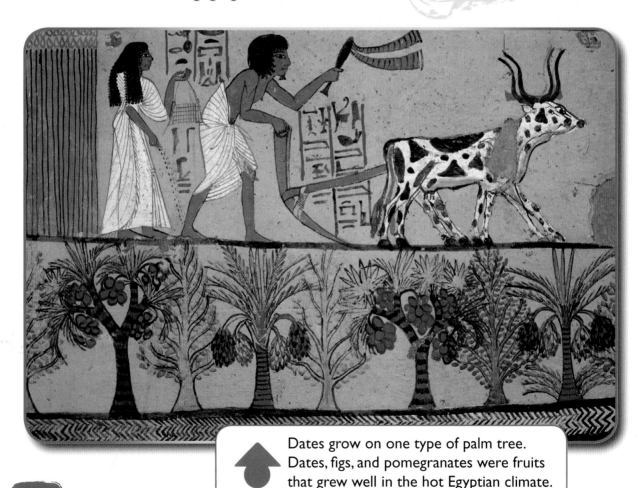

Dates grow on one type of palm tree. Dates, figs, and pomegranates were fruits that grew well in the hot Egyptian climate.

1. Pour honey into a small bowl and mix in ground cinnamon.

2. Place ground almonds in another small bowl.

3. Stuff each date with walnut pieces.

4. Dip each stuffed date in the cinnamon honey to coat, then roll completely in ground almonds.

5. Serve at room temperature. Refrigerate leftovers.

Tiger nut sweets

Tiger nut sweets are finger-food. Instead of using cutlery, ancient Egyptians, simply picked up their food with their fingers.

Activity: Papyrus and hieroglyphs

To make **papyrus**, the Egyptians picked papyrus reeds from the Nile. The outside of the reeds were peeled away and the insides were cut into thin strips. Strips were lined up next to each other. A second layer of strips was placed crosswise. The wet papyrus was then covered with linen and pounded with rocks. The plant's natural juices made the layers stick together. Once the papyrus was dry, it could be used as paper.

Supplies

- PVA glue
- bright poster or acrylic paint and brushes, or oil-based pastels
- sugar paper, or other rough paper
- large salad bowl
- greaseproof or wax paper

Warning!

This project is messy. Protect your clothing and work surface.

Read all directions before beginning the project.

Papyrus was one of the earliest kinds of writing material.

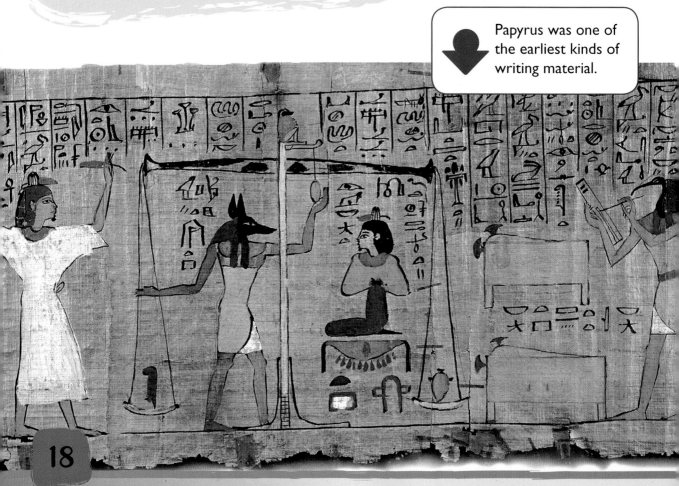

❶ Lay or tape the wax or greaseproof paper down so that your project won't stick to your work surface.

❷ Mix about half a small bottle of white glue with an equal amount of water in a bowl. If you are using paste, water the paste down by using twice as much water as is suggested in its mixing directions.

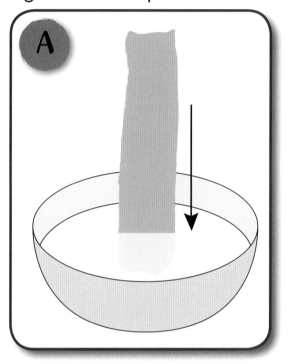

❸ Tear the brown paper bag into strips about 5 centimetres wide. Don't worry if the strips vary in width – jagged ends will bind together better than a clean cut.

❹ Dip one strip of the brown paper into the glue mixture. Make sure you soak it completely – and don't be afraid to get some on your hands! (See Picture A)

❺ When you take out the strip, slide it between your fingers to remove any extra glue mixture. Then place it horizontally on the wax or greaseproof paper.

❻ Repeat this process, dipping another strip, squeezing out the excess, and placing the strip parallel to the first strip. The strips should overlap a little. (See Picture B)

7 Continue this process, placing more and more strips side-by-side until you have used about half of your brown paper. Press down on the strips to make the layer smooth. This is your first layer.

8 To start making your second layer, use another strip, and dip and squeeze it like before. This time place it across the other strips, perpendicular to the first layer. (See Picture C)

9 Continue making more strips and placing them on this new layer.

10 When you have used all of your paper, press down on the strips to make the layers smooth.

11 Let the paper air dry overnight.

12 Once your paper is dry, you can use it. Use a pencil to create your design or message, then make it more permanent with the paints.

What will you draw or write on your paper? How will what you write on this paper differ from what you would write on normal paper or on a computer? What might an Egyptian child write about?

Papyrus with hieroglyphs

Hieroglyphic writing uses pictures, called hieroglyphs, instead of letters to record information or to tell a story.

Activity: *shabti figurines*

Egyptians believed that even after death the gods might require duty work, just like the **pharaoh**. *Shabtis* were figurines painted and buried with the dead. Egyptians believed that these magical statues could do someone's duty work in the **afterlife**. They would be brought to life by a spell when they were needed. The tombs of wealthy people sometimes held a *shabti* worker for each day of the year. Poorer tombs only had a few *shabtis*.

Warning!

Make sure you read all directions before beginning the project.

Supplies

- newspaper
- masking tape
- plaster gauze (available at craft shops) cut into about 20 2.5 cm by 7.5 cm strips
- marker pens

Each *shabti* was labelled with the dead person's name and a spell to bring the statue to life.

1. Use newspaper to create an oblong, mummy-like shape. (See Picture A)

2. Wrap masking tape around the newspaper until the newspaper is completely covered, like a mummy. (See Picture B)

3. Dip strips of plaster gauze into water and use your fingers to remove the excess water. Cover the masking tape with the strips of wet plaster gauze, just like a mummy.

4. Decide what job you will give to your *shabti*.

A

B

What job would you most like your *shabti* to do for you?

⑤ Decorate the face of the *shabti* in the Egyptian style. (See Picture C)

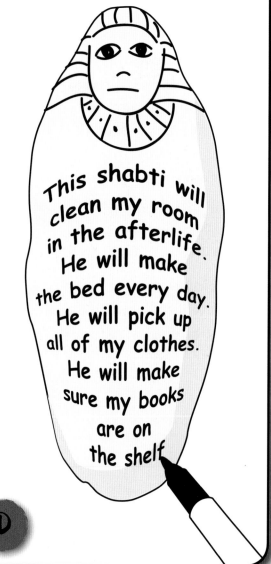

This shabti will clean my room in the afterlife. He will make the bed every day. He will pick up all of my clothes. He will make sure my books are on the shelf

⑥ Use markers to write on the gauze the jobs the *shabti* will do for you. Write as many details as you can so that your *shabti* will know exactly what to do. (See Picture D)

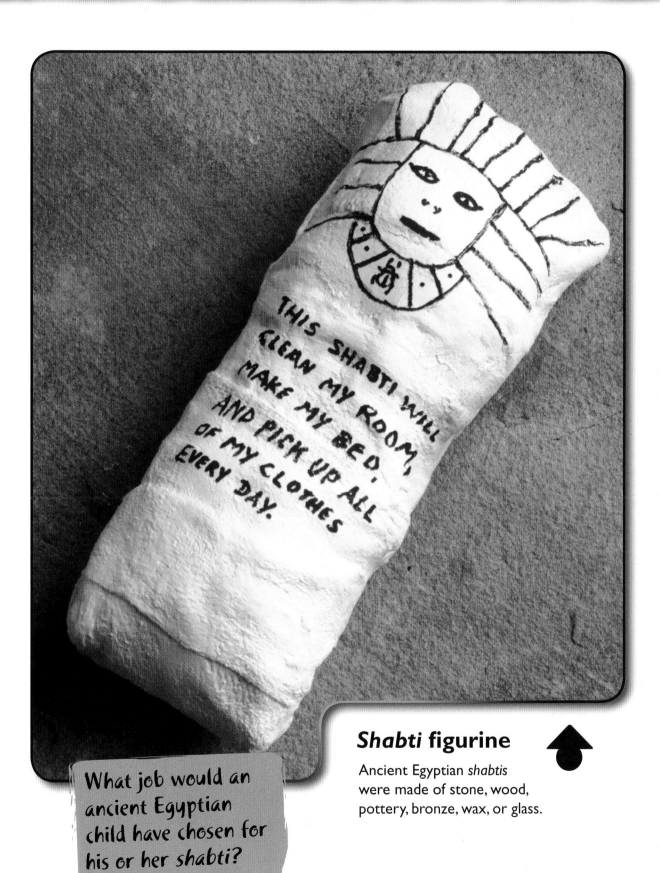

On figurine:

THIS SHABTI WILL CLEAN MY ROOM, MAKE MY BED, AND PICK UP ALL OF MY CLOTHES EVERY DAY.

Shabti figurine

Ancient Egyptian *shabtis* were made of stone, wood, pottery, bronze, wax, or glass.

What job would an ancient Egyptian child have chosen for his or her shabti?

Activity:
Egyptian senet game

Senet was a popular Egyptian board game for children and adults. The name senet means "passing". Senet was played for fun, but it also had a deeper meaning. It might have been played as a symbol of the troubles a soul might have passing to the **afterlife**.

Warning!
Make sure you read all directions before beginning the project.

 Four senet game boards were found in the tomb of Tutankhamun. One was trimmed with pieces of gold, ivory, and silver.

Supplies
- coloured card or regular paper, at least 7.5 cm by 25 cm. Or use the lid from a shoebox.
- ruler
- pencil or marker
- draughts or similarly-sized counters or game pieces in two colours or shapes
- dice or lolly pop sticks

1 On the card, paper, or inside of the shoebox lid, use a ruler and pencil or marker to draw a rectangle measuring 7.5 cm by 25 cm.

2 Along a 7.5 cm-side of the rectangle, measure 2.5 cm and make a mark. Without moving your ruler, measure 5 cm and make another mark.

3 Repeat this process on the other 7.5 cm side, measuring 2.5 cm and 5 cm. (See Picture A)

4 Connect the 2.5 cm marks from one side to the other. Do the same thing with the 5 cm marks, so that you have created three columns, each 2.5 cm wide.

A

B

5 Use the same process to divide your columns into 2.5 cm squares. Measure along one 25 cm line and make marks at every 2.5 cm. Repeat this on a different 25 cm line, marking 2.5 cm. Connect the marks across all three columns. You should now have three columns of ten squares. (See Picture B)

6 Optional step

When you play this game, you will be moving your draughts
or counters around the board. To know how many spaces to
move, you can roll a die. Or, to play a more authentic game, make
throwing sticks to determine how many spaces to move. Draw
an animal head on one side of a lolly pop stick. Make a total of six
sticks, each with a head on one side. Throw the sticks like rolling
dice – the number of heads that land facing up tells you how many
spaces you can move. (See Picture C)

How could you
use more lolly
sticks or other
materials for
playing pieces?
How could you
make Egyptian-
styled pieces?

How to play senet

Number of players: two
Goal: to be the first player to remove all counters from the board

1. Place the draughts in alternate colours down the left-hand side of the board. The players will move their counters up the left-hand column, down the centre column, up the right-hand column, and then off the board. (See Picture D)

2. Throw the sticks or one die to see how far to move. Begin with the counter nearest to the start (the bottom left-hand corner of the board).

3. If you land on a square occupied by one of your own pieces, you can stay. If you land on your opponent's piece, you must go back to the start.

4. Players take turns.

5. When the first counter has passed the finish and is off the board, you start again with the second counter. Continue until all 5 counters are off the board.

End here

D

Start here

Egyptian senet game

29

Glossary

afterlife life or existence after death

canal artificial waterway used for irrigation, drainage, or travel

descendant person or animal who comes later in a family

fertile good for growing

irrigate to water by means of ditches, canals, or pipes

papyrus a material used for writing on

peasants poor workers, often those who do the farm work for someone else who owns the land

pharaoh an ancient Egyptian ruler

More books to read

Arts and Crafts of the Ancient World: Ancient Egypt, Ting Morris (Watts Publishing, 2006)

Excavating the Past: Ancient Egypt, Jackie Gaff (Heinemann Library, 2004)

History Beneath Your Feet: Ancient Egypt, Jane Shuter (Hodder & Stoughton Childrens, 2003)

History Opens Windows: The Ancient Egyptians, Jane Shuter (Heinemann Library, 2006)

Understanding People in the Past: The Ancient Egyptians, Rosemary Rees (Heinemann Library, 2006)

What Families Were Like: Ancient Egypt, Alison Cooper (Hodder & Stoughton Childrens, 2003)

You Are In: Ancient Egypt, Ivan Minnis (Raintree Perspectives, 2004)

The instructions for the crafts and activities are designed to allow pupils to work as independently as possible. However, it is always a good idea to make a prototype before assigning any project so that pupils can see how their own work will look when completed. Prior to introducing these activities, teachers should collect and prepare the materials and be ready for any modifications that may be necessary. Participating in the project-making process will help teachers understand the directions and be ready to assist pupils with difficult steps. Teachers might also choose to adapt or modify the projects to better suit the needs of an individual child or class. No one knows the levels of achievement pupils will reach better than their teacher.

While it is preferable for pupils to work as independently as possible, there is some flexibility in regards to project materials and tools. They can vary according to what is available. For instance, while standard white glue may be most familiar, there might be times when a teacher will choose to speed up a project by using a hot glue gun to join materials. Where plaster gauze is not availabe, papier mâché can often be used. Likewise, while a project may call for leather cord, in most instances it is possible to substitute plastic rope or even wool or string. Acrylic paint may be recommended because it adheres better to a material like felt or plastic, but other types of paint would be suitable as well. Circles can be drawn with a compass, or simply by tracing a cup, roll of tape, or other circular object. Allowing pupils a broad spectrum of creativity and opportunities to problem-solve within the parameters of a given project will encourage their critical thinking skills most fully.

Each project contains a question within the directions. These questions are meant to be thought-provoking and promote discussion while pupils work on the project.

Index

Titles in the *Hands on Ancient History* series include:

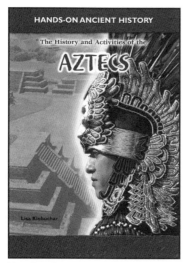

Hardback   978 0 431 08083 3

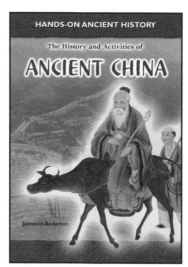

Hardback   978 0 431 08086 4

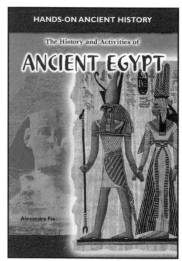

Hardback   978 0 431 08084 0

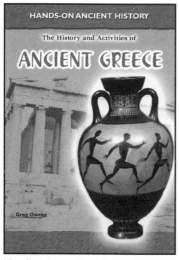

Hardback   978 0 431 08085 7

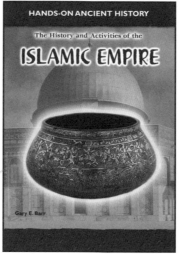

Hardback   978 0 431 08089 5

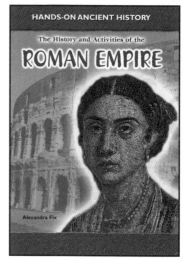

Hardback   978 0 431 08087 1

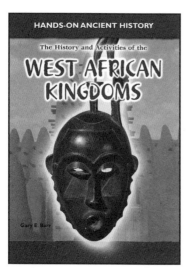

Hardback   978 0 431 08088 8

Find out about other titles from Heinemann Library on our website www.heinemann.co.uk/library